Bleeding Lilies Blooming Bowers

a poetry collection by

Dr.Sudha Subramaniam

Writersgram Publications

Bleeding Lilies Blooming Bowers
by Dr.Sudha Subramaniam

First Impression: July 2021

ISBN: 978-93-91485-93-1

Published by: Writersgram Publications, New Delhi

www.writersgram.com
publications@writersgram.com

Published in India

Maximum Retail Price: ₹ 150.79

Dedication

My heart that has felt and my innermost recesses that have seen and experienced so much, must necessarily surface from its confines to dedicate each and every poem contained in 'Bleeding Lilies Blooming Bowers' at the altar of humanity. I take pleasure in expressing my dedication in prose. Harbouring immense hope, it has been inked for those in whose love I have blossomed and to each and every reader.

Contents

A Singular Drop of Water

The raindrop that refracts the sunlight
Touches the earth to form its oceans;
The rainbow stretching from horizon to horizon
Is an ode to that refraction.

Blue oceans that reflect the rainbow
Ripple in bounded shores with boundless
immensity
While clouds that condense to bring alive
parched earth
Float high above to give water vapour a berth.

Creating a bountiful tomorrow with silent movement
The unseen hand shelters to give birth;
So also, may each one of us tend the humane farm
So that the world we belong to serenely exudes
eternal charm.

Preface

Her crushed form lay on the bed. The fragrance of lilies clothed the air. As the crack of dawn broke the darkness, the slanting windows opened to reveal that she had bled. The colour red coursed through my veins, my hair stood up on end and my eyes became pools of welling tears.

The silent night had stifled her screams and her scars became stories in the lanes of memories. She lived in my verses and screamed through soundless pages. I held a mirror to her shattered dreams and harnessed her feelings through timeless expressions.

Every soul housed in the body seemed like a wingless bird in a cage. My words spilled out to reveal the victims of circumstances and I strived to hold back the limitless outpourings. Every heart that once echoed in the valley of pristine beauty and rose to wing across the free blue skies seemed to metamorphose from buds to blooms. But through the valleys and blooming bowers I had spotted the bleeding lilies.

The lens of my vision zoomed in to reveal thoughts swept with reality and gushing with virginity. From simple joys to complex emotions, I felt my pen etch the reality. As the earth continues its ceaseless spin, as thoughts run into oceans and pens run dry, as crying hearts hide behind smiling lips, as the dipping Sun is enveloped by the blanket of night, as lilies bloom to spread fragrance and joy, the words still come alive and live on to tell...that every poem is not the same. Words will be words and hearts will be strung; to cry out in verse, to spell out the truth.

I implore my readers to join with me in realising the hidden beauty that is so sacred and to take pleasure in the poetry that is but an expression of thoughts and feelings drawn from imagination as well as from reality.

Dr.Sudha Subramaniam

Introduction

So as the plumule pushes its way up from the soil that nourishes and then grows onwards, my initial writings were written closer to my beginnings. As I continued to perpetually bask in the wealth of words, I aspired to express the seen and the unseen. That which is beholden beauty strove to immortalise dreams etched in the mind's vision. That which is a flow sought to crystallise the journey's pathways. 'Hathras Shame' has been written with my blood boiling and hair standing on end. As the media zoomed in on the horrifying incident my rational mind could not help but ask me, 'Why isn't there greater security interwoven into the machinery so as to have continuous police patrolling? After all, we do have that incredible human capital". 'Her Odyssey' signifies hope amidst the torment. 'Enveloped in Love' can have hidden meanings and the writer's pen seeks to express the varied dimensions of human existence that is much more than just compartmentalised love. 'Harijan' is a fluid expression of the history of discrimination. 'Reminiscence' casts me in a lingering fragrance of blooming bowers that I strive to clutch on to but then the lily is bleeding again as 'Doomsday' has been triggered. 'Drunken Ordeal' marks inescapable occurrences of endless pain and offers a beacon light by suggesting that the victims of circumstances could gather courage to overcome and break free. 'Chance Meeting' spells out the bigger picture of philanthropy and poverty with striking truth. 'Lost Love' is that poignant realisation of the glory of love that bonded two lovers while 'The Christmas that was' and 'My Dad Lives Forever' is an expression of Dad's unequivocal love. 'Following My Heart' and 'Swinging with You' are outpourings that recollect and seek the company of loved ones.

'Covid-19', 'The Killing Fields', 'Discrimination', 'Immigrant', 'Black' and 'Special Moments' are rooted in reality. As the heart opens out, so also 'Demystifying Creation', 'Towering Truth', 'Behold', 'Mirror', 'Dream' and 'Friend' are echoes of the mind that is incessantly searching for the truth of creation, for greater dimensions of beauty and for true friendship.

As shed tears and unshed tears continue to spill for the bleeding lilies, so also the seeking mind demystifies creation's bounty that blooms in hidden bowers.

Dr.Sudha Subramaniam

Acknowledgement

My journey so far in the path of education, writing and the art of being human has been marked with diverse and enriching experiences. First and foremost, I acknowledge the creator and the creation that has empowered me to write. I am grateful for the encouragement and support from my family as I strayed into the garden of thoughts to pluck from the trees of imagination rooted in reality. I express my heartfelt and bounden remembrances for the role of my grandparents, my father and other elders who nourished me with beautiful thoughts, words and deeds and who are now in their heavenly abode. My father had given the title, 'Edges' for my first poem. I acknowledge the continuing love and support of my mother Jayalakshmi, my husband Subramaniam my children Radha and Rohan. I acknowledge the affection of my vast and adorable family and extended family. I also express my thankfulness for the legacy given to me by the writers in our family, the famed poet and writer Parapalli Krishna Iyer and the famous Engineer-writer Dr.Kocha. I also express my profound gratitude to every forum and to every platform that provided the springboard for me to grow to greater heights. I further acknowledge the valuable contribution of the freedom-fighters of our family whose valour and dedication contributed towards the carving of a free India from where we could embark on our voyage of discovery and development.

I acknowledge the immense value-addition to literature and to literary genius that Writersgram has provided through this valuable initiative of publishing and I am extremely thankful to Mr.Ramesh Kumar, Director, Publications, of Writersgram and the entire team of Writersgram Publications. Indeed, Writersgram has made many a beautiful dream possible.

Dr.Sudha Subramaniam

Brief Biosketch Of Author

Dr.Sudha Subramaniam, M.Com, M.Phil, PhD, Med, CA Final Group I, a Professor-Educator and a writer, was born in June 1966 in Kottayam, Kerala. Brought up in Mumbai and a regular visitor to her native place, her love for India and everything Indian is deep-rooted. A childhood spent growing up with Amar Chitra Katha, Chandamama, Fairy Tales, Bedtime Tales, Indian Epics, stories of the Temples of India, Enid Blyton, Russian, American and German authors as well, forged her literary roots and embedded the love for expressing through writing. Sudha is a regular writer and has written several articles and poems for the Bhavans Journal including the well-known Vikram and Betaal contemporary series; has written for leading newspapers and editions, has a book of poems published by Bharatiya Vidya Bhavan titled, 'The Dawn of Creation', which was selected as the 'Best book of the Fortnight', writes poems on Indian epics and mythology and has won the award from Bharatiya Vidya Bhavan for her poem 'Draupadi's Invincible Faith'. Sudha's poem, 'Learning Forgiveness from the Mahabharata' has been translated into Kannada. She has also co-authored the book on 'Hundred Greatest Wealth Creators of India' and is the recipient of the prestigious 'Outstanding Contribution for Research-ORCA Award' from the University of Mumbai. Sudha is also the recipient of the Asian Literary Society's Wordsmith Award of Excellence in Poetry writing and the 2021 winner of the Sagar Memorial Award for Literature.

With several awards and accolades to her credit in diverse speres including community service, Sudha has anchored herself in the amazing literary sphere and has been a panelist at literary and at research forums. Her mainstay is that reading and writing hold the key to the bountiful and evergreen blooming of one's inner self.

Sudha would love to stay connected with readers on sdhsubramaniam21@gmail.com

Hathras Shame

Her formless figure rose from the ashes
Hovering over the perpetrators of sin;
From mutilated body to putrified carcass
She withstood the torment of agony.
Blameless wide innocent eyes sunk forever
In the ocean that has lost its virginity;
Clouds of anguish swirling over yesterday,
A melancholy hurricane in the vast abyss of today.
An endless darkness outside the tunnel of
victimisation
As headlines proclaimed the gruesome coercion;
The spring of her life pinned down by violence,
Forlorn autumn holding a bloom crushed
without defence.
Yearning to be held in the arms of her mother,
To be clothed anew with dresses bought by father,
But Alas! The naked truth is written forever
In the form of a skeleton that outlived the
bloody horror.
While the consuming fire rages and billows into a blaze
Nameless shame rises to cloak the human race.
For she died to live in the petrified annal
Of decried abuse and exploiting for pleasures carnal.

Her Odyssey

A solitary tear rolled down her cheek
From the lurking shadows of yesterday;
A memory that choked out future joy,
Mind scarred by an evil ploy.
Like a rolling wave skirting the vast shore,
She sought refuge in the ocean of humanity.
A fluff of white cloud dotting the blue sky
Reflected in the boundless waters
Touched that single wave and rode along its crest
Challenging the infinity above to keep abreast;
While surfacing tears from deep pools
Settled in the reservoir of shackled thoughts;
Till yesterday's shadows dissolved in today's sunbeams,
Sorrowful memories effaced with tomorrow's dreams.
A hand reached out to clasp hers firmly
To guide her through pathways lit dimly;
Beyond the bend lay a new journey
Meeting the road onwards to glory.
The shore embraced the rolling wave
While a new horizon bowed to meet the brave.

Enveloped in Love

As the melting wax clung to the edges of the candle
The velvet night draped itself along the
pathways of my sight;
While the billowing curtains opened out to the
vast expanse of sky,
Gently the moonbeams peeped in with the cool breeze,
Artistically silvering the greens of tall trees.
As moments stretched out in longing
intoxicating
In each other's arms we cruised the stars shining.
A touch of intimacy, a caress of care,
Hearts intertwined to lay love bare.
Lost in divine sensation,
Souls stirring to cosmic beating
In realms of ecstatic awakening.
As traces of candle-wax trailed the diminishing night,
Mingling with the tresses let down by dawn's
first light.

Harijan

Scavenging the garbage, she inched along
From tattered childhood to famished youth;
The creases on her mother's face marked by age
Spoke of time spent in poverty's cage.
Stretched over two poles a sheltering sheet,
Home on the pavement for daily retreat.
Birth gave her the identity, 'Dalit';
Gandhiji called them, 'Harijan'
But seventy years had passed her mother
As time had turned the corner
To hail the arrival of welfare and development,
Firing the belly of the poor.
Words to explain inequality and discrimination
Just fragile forms of expression
Trapped in devastation.
While the wheel seemed to move on
Through the quicksand of situation
Victims of circumstance, of inaction.
Human rights and dignity of labour
Rose out of the pages of the globalised world
Thorns of casteism shred apart
Cast into pages of legal lore.
While she picked out the scrap to recycle
Humanity awaited redressal.

Reminiscence

Seated on the corner bench of our garden
Where fragrant lilies abound on tender stems
Red mud holds close the emerging glory
My eyes reflecting blooming rhapsody;
Birdsong mellifluous and vibrating resonates
While parrots screech through in musical beats.
Gently catching the flitting butterflies
I conquer the urge to keep them close
Releasing orange, yellow and spotted blue
To converge in the stream of white,
My heart a pathway of reminiscence
At the corner seat of luminescence.
Banyan tree emanating sunbeams of care
'Neath its gaze we played ludo and cards;
As we emerged from childhood's peripheries
Sailing into beckoning youth's glories
Spreading branches tumbled shade in a heap
Strong roots of friendship running deep.
Coursing through years as times evolved
Life's garden stretched into the beyond
On far-away soils I plunged to emerge
As an achiever who made his mark in the world.
Moving onwards through the canopy of time
Heart-strings ring with memories sublime.

Doomsday

Galloping towards the endless abyss
Without a clue of tomorrow's pain,
She embellished her nails in utter disdain
Into the once venerated mud of her motherland,
To bring out chemical dirt that strangulated.
Emptiness pitched into the vast space,
Nothingness ascending from spirals of
exploitation.
Writhing pains of a sheltered cocoon
That lost its confines to wanton destruction
Plague consuming mankind now seeking
retribution.
Crouching carnage of tender feelings
Crushed beneath craving and materialism;
Resentment brewing in an overgrown platter
Mirroring the booming hold of deception and
betrayal.
Truth long lost in frenzied politicisation
Etching the lament of millenniums to come,
History will remember the pitfalls of humanity
Castaways from long-lost ships of voyage
Melting into the folds of an unknown
destination
Marred by the making of our own creation.

Drunken Ordeal

Flowing onto the mud floor
From the gash on the calf
Where the hurled knife had pierced,
Blood as silent witness coursed.
Unlocking fresh waves of pain
Without a care to watch the colour drain
From her face so pretty and delicate
Drunken demeanour smote to devastate;
Rasping breath reeking of alcohol
He then caught her hair and flung her down.
While the night grew darker
Her cries grew louder
Enduring Interminable torture.
Brutal, bizarre, existence
Lamenting life's barbarism,
Seeking resurrection of the spirit
Flagged and flayed by oppression.
Till rising to deal with courage and grit
She moved the court to protect her right
Demanded that justice deal with vicious might.
Pinning hope on living with dignity
Free to inhale the sweetness of liberty
Waves of the heart breaking on shores of expectancy.
Pulled out from the depths of hell
Awaiting a dawn powered by will;
Golden sunrays no longer cringing from red
But seamlessly reaching out to heal where she bled.

Chance Meeting

Fingers numb with biting cold
Gingerly treading on the cobbled road
Pushing chilled feet further into her shoes
She approached the beggars huddled together.
Eyes peeping out through torn blankets
Face sunken with deprivation into bony frames
She could see that thin line melting into nothing
The brink of existence holding on to subsistence.
Placing a food packet on hands stretched out
She weaved her way with providential grace
Till a gentle tug on the edge of her dress
Made her halt and turn to behold a young lad
Almost hidden in the gap of a cracked pipe
Discarded amongst the garbage dumps.
Her head on his lap, her grey hair spilling out
He sheltered the pale frame fraught with age.
An imploring hand stretched out for a share
Other hand wound around the old lady in care.
Waxing benevolence, she placed a packet
Then moved onwards with firm purpose.
As she returned to board her waiting car
Yet again she came upon the crack in the pipe;
As the young lad wiped the old lady's mouth
Then put her to sleep with a lullaby of love
She froze at the altar of sheer realisation.

He was rich who gave without having anything
She had become richer not by giving
They had made her richer by accepting;
Experiencing the glow of true compassion
She realised that she had given him only one packet;
But she found her faith in mankind revived
The lad who starved so that his grandmother
survived.

Lost Love

Her euphoric heart once beat in his arms,
Langurous frame entwined in rhapsodical realms
Melting with passion beyond dreams;
Timeless outleash of elevated feelings,
Love from the core
How their spirits did soar!!

Curved long lashes fringing almond brown eyes,
Revealing unfathomable depths of belonging
Endlessly they reached out with craving;
A slice of time indelible,
Their starry nights a parable.

Left alone, hugging close his memories,
The bundle of yesterday's dreams
Spilling out in rhymes,
Embalming forever his lost love's story
In words that lips once planted on hearts;
Beyond yesterday's boundaries
That once encased tomorrow's promise.

The Christmas that was

The tree of my dreams glowed in the light
Reflecting myriad decorations in the night
The sweet scent of pine wafted through the air
Mixing with the music of Jingle Bells.
Weaving fragrance into timeless lyrics
Rudolph the red-nosed reindeer pulled Santa's sleigh
Riding along Lapland on Christmas Day
Bringing back memories of yesterday.
The package tied with red ribbon bore my name
I bent and picked it up from the bounties of time
Held it close before I untied the knot.
I saw him running across the sheets of snow falling
As I stood in the doorway watching
Till he hugged me, lifted me off the ground
Swirled me around, threw me up in the air
Caught me back in his arms
My laughter rippling in peals
Carrying with the cool breeze
To linger forever amongst the trees.
I was his heart-throb, he was my hero!
I glimpse him ride through the Arctic Circle
From Rovaniemi set in the heart of Finland;
A package tied with ribbon held close to heart
He comes through the chimney and places it for me.
I relive the moments of childhood afresh
I can feel time dissolve and melt like the ice.
As I waltz the floor of life with zest
I remember you Daddy; you gave me the very best.

Following My Heart

My eyes captured the candlelight
Spilling onto the deepest recesses of her being
From whence the glow lit up my heart.
Her tears spilled on to the canvas of my painting
Creating hidden rivulets of emotion
That gave life to the sketches I made,
Strokes of varied colour from a palette of
perfection.
She held her thoughts in the palm of her hand
Blew them into words that rode on waves of
feelings;
Stars twinkling within my eyes through strung
clouds drifting,
Heart dancing to the cadence of flights of birds
chirping
The song her heart sings for me through the
throng tapping.
Streams flowing onwards to rivers led
Creating beautiful pathways on which I tread,
Every step closer to merging with the ocean.
Tumultuous love blazed a trail of belonging
A fire that consumed with wistful yearning.

Swinging with You

My formless being waited longingly
To be seated beside you, swinging carefree
Your graceful hand holding onto one carved
brass chain
While your almond shaped eyes look into mine;
Peals of laughter interspersing our chatter
As the breeze picks up strands of our banter.
Oscillating back and forth in rhythmic motion,
My heart winging out in joyful abandon
Movement beyond gravity, timeless ecstasy,
Unlocking feelings of adoration, of perpetual love
Basking now in moments long craved
Bounded by duties and chores of routine
Endless days that merged with time.
As academic pursuits, friends and work
Kept you engrossed as you grew
Beyond the protective shell of home and hearth,
An achiever in the vast, wide world.
Looking on with pride I perceive the endless rainbow
Spanning the skies and refracting white light;
Through every drop of water that I behold
The mystery of sunlight seems to astound;
Raindrops from pristine heights spelling out a message
To look within and unearth the truth
As formless vapour rises to the skies to condense
My being shall one day emerge to create
Vibrations from heartbeats that propitiate.

My Dad Lives Forever

He looked at me so lovingly
With a gaze that spoke volumes
A slender tendril of lily,
I clambered up the wall of life
Sheltered 'neath the glorious skies of home;
Where sunshine from his heart
Nurtured us with affection,
Watered us with dedication,
Held us in everlasting warmth,
Plucking out the thorns from our path.
I waited for him to come
From holding my hands as I took my first steps
To securing my admission at college,
He was always there forever
Towering above bricks and mortar.
I am here in this moment
When he bought me a new pair of shoes
Walk on, he said, to the future of your dreams.
I walk on to relive my moments with him
As I voyage onwards, I behold the winning smile
As I stumble, I feel his hands holding me strong.
I have realised the truth in unfolding memory
Accompanying me through my journey.

Covid-19

When will I walk carefree into my own home,
Enter at will and surprise with a hug?
To come close to my people I fear,
Perhaps I am an asymptomatic carrier.
Spiked virus lurking unseen
Have I become a weed in my own garden?
My mirror reflects the family tree
But I perceive a crack within me
A passive onlooker seeking to erase
An unfamiliar path depriving meeting space.
Alas! Time has warped into quarantine
As normalcy awaits a successful vaccine;
Gone is the fragrance of bowers I knew
Sunset of my Planet has claimed the morning dew.
No longer do the fields of ripe corn beckon
For sight is clouded by alien perception;
The net is cast and man is a prisoner
In his own land he is no longer the master.
A singular thorn has taken many lives
I watch forlorn as the enemy deprives;
Come again sweet times ringing in joy anew
Let me journey in peace to the home where I grew.

Demystifying Creation

Beyond the boundaries of the human frame
My mind journeyed to the abode of the celestials
To delve into the ancient truth of the Universe,
To trace the journey that began eons ago.
I missed the pulsating warmth of the Sun
Through endless darkness of Space
Yet saw an orange ball rising among the hills below
Snow mountains changing in hue to a rosy glow
Before donning a dazzling golden flow.
Like sand dunes changing with the wind
Clouds sailed beneath my gaze.
Like a mermaid rising from the oceans
The constellation of Pisces rose to greet.
Red sky of Mars and orange of Venus
Transitioning from blue to turquoise behold Uranus.
Yellow to orange to brown the mysterious
Saturn's moon
Slowly moves around a golden sky with a stripe.
Meandering through the constellation of Sagittarius
Catching the arrow shooting from the bow,
I bumped into the twins of Gemini
Bewitching constellations trailing me.
Winging into distant solar systems
As I traversed through time warped in a black hole,
I peeped out to see a Star explode.
Winding along the seemingly endless tunnel
I spilled out into yesterday through the funnel.
A huge aura of stardust greeted my eyes

Shooting colours through huge bridges of ice
Slowly breaking to form chunks of matter
Hurtling along into a cosmic platter.
Balls of unscathing fire came roaring on oceans of silver
Waves of different colours rolled on with silent whisper;
Rising spirals of ethereally billowing blue vapour
Danced around me in primordial caper.
I held on to an emerging vine of green
To behold a transformation intensely serene;
The twinkling bands of coloured dust
Interlaced with the waves to encrust
Bonded together to create a nest
As creation huddled in mighty quest.

Towering Truth

Gently the evening rises to melt into the night
Twinkling with mystery the stars converse;
Stretching upwards trees open out their hearts
Gazing to unravel treasures from hidden heights.
Carrying a message from Andromeda afar
A shooting star becomes a voyageur
Sailing along the pathways on a cloud
Speaking out my thoughts aloud,
Watching the ocean of milk unfold
Gazing at starlings with luminescence endowed.
The hidden path that lay between the sea of clouds
Parting to reveal the submerged road unfold;
Through lanterns of memories illuminating the mind,
My aura searching amidst the skies seeks to find
The golden gate that had appeared to astound
A sight which I beheld spellbound;
When innocence still bore its stamp on my life
When the pages of my book were not strewn with strife;
When darkness of the night carried silver wings
To fly onwards into the dreams that every
morning brings.
As childhood questioned and youth blossomed
As craving knowledge new horizons welcomed,
The force that pulled me to unravel many a mystery
Meanders along the towers of history.

The Killing Fields

Sweat from his brow wet the soil
As the bullocks ploughed and he held on
Sunburnt and strong he tilled with care
Land of his forefathers, good harvest would bear.
Nights of revelry dancing around the fire
Tapping feet, clapping hands, laughing eyes;
The breeze gently whispered into the ears of corn
Ready to harvest, crops unfurled the morn.
But alas!! The moneylender oppressed and took his dues
Leaving heavy hearts, poverty rearing to suffuse;
Till came the day when two brothers parted ways
One continued to farm, one went out of the maze
He landed in the urban sprawl
Up the labourer's ladder began his crawl.
Gradually his bank account rose to three and four digits
Some funds he could send to his village home;
But the moneylender's noose grew stronger still
A vicious circle, beyond body and will.
With families to care, disparity increased
One had more than his fill, one had only land to till.
The farmer felt himself a failure, he craved for death;
He hung himself, soul escaping with a final breath.

Discrimination

Who are you to take away my self-respect,
To put yourself on a high pedestal?
I see myself as a person in my own right
I will not bow to your position or might.
If you treat me with warmth and love
You can win my heart and befriend.
Behold the tall tree laden with fruits
Owes its existence to strong roots;
The sailor rows as the ship seeks the shore
Rippling with care, hearts unlock humanity's door;
Extend your vision with wisdom to see
Beneath the blue skies I am born free.
Black or white, blood flows red
Stuff within is what makes a purebred;
Why should man against man be pitted
Without disgrace and disdain let's be committed
To bloom with glory in the garden of life
Without being ravaged by pests of strife.
Do not commit acts of hatred and violence gory
For tomorrow will lie in ruins as a sad story
Fossils of mankind etched in rock
Will live to tell, let not time mock.

Behold

Do you see the wind that moves the leaves
Sunlight through miles of dark space traverse
Buds that open out to the touch of dawn
Dewdrops that settle on the blooms of morn
Valleys that echo with the call of hills
Breaking silence, birds gracefully taking to wings.
Gushing springs, flowing streams, cascading waterfalls
Drenched in dappling beauty, nature's canvas enthralls.
Rustic song on his *ektara* the nomad strumming
Travellers lured to a mirage of an oasis, thirsting
In vast sand dunes desert endlessly stretching
Water in bagpipes, camel caravans meandering.
Orange Sun gently dipping into waters now darker
Stars twinkling through light years in
constellations stellar.
Shadows that lengthen with the onset of twilight
Merging, disappearing, into the darkness of
night.

Mirror

May I ask you a question
And expect an answer;
Or may I look deeper and reflect
On the properties of matter
Subterfuged in simplicity,
Harbouring vitality
With vivid captures
Carved in perfection,
Instant creation,
A marvellous reflection.
As close as touch
As far as the eye can see
You mesmerise me
With an internal existence
Of external reality;
Just an image of me
Forever there when I see.
Mirror on the wall
Catching the change
Gently pronouncing
Time and age.

Dream

My dream perched on the window sill
Gazing at the mesmerising star spangled view
Engulfing evening with crimson sunset hue
The deep velvet night had its fill.
A tiny speck of thought unfurled
Laying out an endless carpet
Of beautiful aspirations that beget
Imagination leading to endless search.
Not knowing whether to take off from the perch
Or whether to just remain a thought,
I looked within and answers sought
I delved within and expressed in prose.
Then the sudden crack of dawn arose
My dream went sailing off in the morning light;
I tried my best to keep it in sight
To hold it to my bosom close.
I could feel the splatter
When the oar touched the water,
I could feel the lilt of the river;
Listened to the overhanging murmur,
The resonance of nature's choir.
Where do the waves begin?
Where do the ripples end?
Are there hidden caverns behind the waterfalls?
Treasures in the water's depths?
Basking in hidden grottos,
Drinking in the luxurious freshness
Of sea breeze tangled in pine and mangoes

Waltzing through lilies, exacums and ixoras.
My tiffin of boiled tapioca and green chillies
Wrapped in plantain leaf, now unpacked;
My tastebuds lingered on every morsel
A forever ride in my life's dossier.
I looked up at the slanting beams
Of sunshine filtering through window panes
Road-mapping life's many lanes
My dreams ascended to surrealistic realms.

Friend

Could I confide something
And trust you to support me;
Would you know my real self
Without suspecting misplaced intentions?
Could I share my sorrows and grief
And get your shoulder to cry on?
Would you speak well of me
And feel the joys I feel?
Would you understand where my shoe pinches,
Would you care to know the paths I tread?
Could I have a right to your time
And let you take mine;
Do you want to wipe my tears,
Smile with me in delight?
If the food is burnt would you rather
Bandage my bruised finger?
If you feel the pangs of hunger
Will you wait for my company that you treasure?
Could we spend endless hours
Picking shells on golden beaches,
Flying kites that span the blue above,
Watch the Kingfishers dive into the water,
Peep together into nature's bower;
Listen to the echo from the valleys of belonging
The bond between life and the heart beating;
Joy resonating, care pulsating;
True friendship vibrating
A beautiful relationship, forever abiding.

Immigrant

The Statue of Liberty stands for me
The dollar's strength powered by me
So what if I am an immigrant?
I have shaped the USA!!
I am the soul of the great scientist Einstein
I am the co-founder of Google,
game-changer Sergei Brin;
Wear my jeans, I am Levi Strauss
Write about me, bag the Pulitzer.
So what if I am an immigrant?
I have shaped the USA.
I run into pages and pages
Having worked for ages
My blood has toiled and tilled
To yield fortunes coffers filled.
Never building walls nor breeding hate
The future with time is my date.
It has taken me years to create
What you can never emulate
For the sweat in my brow will stay
The denizens of tomorrow will say;
So what if I am an immigrant
Your very greatness my complement.

Black

The tiny 'Black' girl
Held on to my tresses
As dense as my African tribal jungle;
Where silent sentinels guarded our customs,
Modernisation considered taboo.
Haunted by the ghosts of her past,
She gingerly treads the bridge
Reaching out to a brighter future;
With the hem of her attire
Stuck to yesterday's road.
Now in the land of whites
She carries her stamp;
Surfacing from the quagmire,
She walked the ramp
To success.
The colour of her skin is a barrier no more,
Her blood flows red from shore to shore.
Humanity embellished with education
Has illumined deep within.

Special Moments

Like a figment of imagination
Marking a momentous occasion;
He stretched out to me,
Face mirroring his passion;
Holding the young one
In the palms of his hands.
My thumbs wound around the tender frame,
Alert to the slightest movements;
Holding him firm, taking small steps forward;
The water's edge playing with my garments,
Leading me onwards,
Trailing the sands.
As endless waves enthralled the calm seas,
Golden hues in shimmering shafts shone,
Clasping the young one with loving firmness,
I gazed transfixed as the waters flowed on.
Gently bent and released the little one
To clamber on all fours,
Disappear into the beckoning blues.
I had released the radiated turtle
From the confines of cared breeding,
Into the vastness of the biosphere;
Playing a role in heeding
The need for conservation of species;
An enshrined moment of existence.